RAND NATIONAL DEFENSE RESEARCH INSTITUTE

T0097356

Authorities for Military Operations Against Terrorist Groups

The State of the Debate and Options for Congress

Christopher S. Chivvis, Andrew M. Liepman

Prepared for the Office of the Secretary of Defense

Approved for public release; distribution unlimited

For more information on this publication, visit www.rand.org/t/RR1145-1

Library of Congress Cataloging-in-Publication Data is available for this publication.
ISBN: 978-0-8330-9079-9

Published by the RAND Corporation, Santa Monica, Calif.
© Copyright 2016 RAND Corporation
RAND® is a registered trademark.

Cover image: A pair of F-16 Fighting Falcons on a mission in August. The aircraft are assigned to the 332nd Air Expeditionary Wing at Balad Air Base, Iraq (U.S. Air Force photo by Tech. Sgt. Scott Reed).

Support RAND
Make a tax-deductible charitable contribution at
www.rand.org/giving/contribute

www.rand.org

Preface

This report surveys the debate over the requirements for a new congressional authorization for the use of military force (AUMF). It captures the results of two workshops, an extensive literature review, and consultations with senior experts and practitioners in the executive branch and Congress. The first of the two RAND-organized workshops, in November 2014, brought together experts on the global threat environment to examine the evolution of the terrorist threat and its likely trajectory. The second, in February 2015, elicited the perspectives of legal and policy experts, focusing on specific elements of notional versions of a congressional AUMF. We thus sought to survey the current thinking among both terrorism and legal experts to gauge the spectrum of views on the subject, ascertain the most important elements of such an authorization, and, by adding our own insights on counterterrorism operations and the threat trajectory, offer options to help inform the congressional debate on an AUMF. In doing so, we were cognizant that the debate was shifting and that congressional support for a new AUMF was fluctuating. In the midst of our effort, the White House submitted to Congress its own draft authorization—essentially providing a specific proposal to test against the theoretical models constructed for this study but also rendering the subject even more politically charged than in the past. We remain mindful of these political realities while also presenting an objective, nonpartisan view of possible directions and implications for an AUMF from a broad national security perspective.

This research was sponsored by the Office of the Secretary of Defense and conducted within the International Security and Defense Policy Center of the RAND National Defense Research Institute, a federally funded research and development center sponsored by the Office of the Secretary of Defense, the Joint Staff, the Unified Combatant Commands, the Navy, the Marine Corps, the defense agencies, and the defense Intelligence Community.

For more information on the International Security and Defense Policy Center, see www.rand.org/nsrd/ndri/centers/isdp or contact the director (contact information is provided on the web page).

Contents

Summary

Most U.S. military operations against terrorist groups are conducted under authorities Congress granted the executive branch after the September 11, 2001, terrorist attacks in the form of an authorization for the use of military force (AUMF).[1] That authorization is broadly worded to cover a range of counterterrorism operations. It has, moreover, been interpreted to cover a similarly broad range of terrorist groups. As of mid-2016, the AUMF remained an effective authorization for most of the country's counterterrorism needs.

Relying on the 2001 authorization is far from ideal, however, and Congress could update the legislation to better reflect the current counterterrorism challenge. The 2001 authorization is clearly linked to the perpetrators of the 9/11 attacks, many of whom have been eliminated. The need for counterterrorism operations clearly continues, but key groups the United States faces are no longer those that posed the greatest threat in 2001. Operations can continue under the 2001 authority, but not without legal gymnastics in some cases.

To provide a clearer legal authority for current counterterrorism operations, Congress should consider passing new legislation to reflect this changed environment and underscore U.S. determination to counter these new threats—in addition to any older ones that remain. Doing so would send a clear message about United States' commitment to future counterterrorism operations and offer a clearer and more ratio-

---

[1] Public Law 107-40, Joint Resolution to Authorize the Use of United States Armed Forces Against Those Responsible for the Recent Attacks Launched Against the United States, September 18, 2001.

nal overall framework for such operations going forward. The passage and enactment of a new AUMF would signal agreement between the legislative and the executive branches on this issue and would telegraph continued U.S. resolve and help clarify for the American public and the world the severity and character of today's counterterrorism challenge. In contrast, a failure to pass new legislation, especially given the debate that has occurred in Congress, could send the signal that the U.S. will to fight terrorist groups has dwindled in the nearly 15 years since 9/11.

As of mid-2016, the Islamic State of Iraq and the Levant (ISIL) had been responsible for multiple terrorist attacks outside Iraq and Syria. It claimed credit for and Russia has concluded that ISIL was responsible for the downing of the Russian airliner over Egypt, which killed more than 200 people, and Russia has subsequently greatly increased its military involvement in Syria. In Paris, the group organized a series of large-scale attacks that killed more than 130; in Brussels, attacks killed 32. France insisted that it would never buckle to terrorist pressure, and the country launched airstrikes on ISIL's headquarters in Syria. Although the group has not claimed responsibility, Turkey alleges that ISIL was behind attacks in the Istanbul airport, and the two lone-wolf attacks in the United States—in Orlando, Florida, and San Bernardino, California—were both at least partly motivated by ISIL's ideology.

The United States, partly in response to this increasingly lethal global terrorist campaign, has ratcheted up its military operations against ISIL. Limited air assaults have reaped some success, including the destruction of a sizable fleet of fuel trucks and oil production facilities, incinerating large cash stockpiles, facilitating Kurdish advances in both Syria and Iraq, and helping Iraqi forces retake large chunks for territory from ISIL, including Ramadi and, most recently, Fallujah. However, these responses represent slow and painstaking progress in the face of increasingly aggressive and lethal attacks. Even before the attack in Paris and the downing of the Russian plane, the United States started to put its foot on the gas pedal, promising to increase the frequency and power of airstrikes, sending limited special forces units to

Syria to assist with intelligence and targeting, and upping its assistance to the Kurds.

These moves seem sensible in the face of a worsening threat. The need to dismantle ISIL's terrorist and military capacity has gained new urgency. But the shifting battle strategy also presents an opportunity for Congress to weigh in—to add its voice to the calls for a strong response to the growing threat from ISIL. The need for a new AUMF was clear when the air war began; it is now even more important that the newly focused military posture gain a more muscular and tailored legislative underpinning.

This report captures the main lines of debate over congressional authorization for counterterrorism operations and the terrorist challenge to which any such legislation should respond. It also outlines the purposes of such legislation, offers suggestions about key elements of the legislation, and assesses congressional options.

Legislation should reflect the constitutional prerogatives of both the legislative and executive branches and signal U.S. will to bring the full force of the law to bear on the most daunting terrorism challenges. We describe six key elements that Congress may wish to consider in a new authorization: (1) no geographical limitations, because the enemy it targets is geographically diffuse; (2) no limits on the use of ground forces; (3) a fairly broad definition of targeted terrorist groups and their associates to ensure that the AUMF accurately describes the current threat while accommodating the threat's likely evolution; (4) specified purposes for which military force may be used; (5) a requirement to report to Congress on groups that have been targeted under the authority; and (6) a renewal clause to ensure that the AUMF is periodically revisited.

Renewal clauses—so-called sunset provisions—are important not because the contest with terrorist groups will be won or lost in a set period of time but because such clauses provide an opportunity to reinvigorate and update the authorization with new legitimacy at regular intervals. History suggests that terrorist threats evolve and, therefore, so should U.S. authorities.

Were Congress to pass new legislation, it would make the most sense to repeal the 2002 authorization for the Iraq War and establish a provision for sunsetting the 2001 AUMF targeting the parties responsible for the 9/11 attacks. Rescinding these prior authorizations would be symbolic, but would likely have a very positive public messaging effect. More importantly, it might be a necessary part of a political deal to get updated authorities in the first place. That said, not rescinding these authorities would not be measurably detrimental to national security.

Even though new authorization is desirable, Congress may fail to pass new legislation altogether. In that case, the executive branch would likely continue using the 2001 AUMF as its authority to conduct counterterrorism operations. Clearly, any attempt to rescind these existing authorizations without passing an appropriate, new authorization would be a dangerous strategic miscalculation.

Because the United States is likely to continue counterterrorism operations with or without a new authorization, the issue is ultimately less about whether the President can use force against ISIL or any other terrorist group than it is about demonstrating congressional approval—and fostering broader public backing—for such efforts. The White House would clearly prefer to have congressional authorization for its wars, even if it is widely recognized that the executive branch has authority to use force without congressional authorization and there is long historical precedent for so doing. Congressional authorization facilitates the use of force and telegraphs to U.S. adversaries that the country is unwavering in its commitment to fight them until they are no longer a threat to national security.

We anticipate a need for an AUMF for the foreseeable future: The next Congress and the next administration will both face the challenge of matching military necessity with existing congressional authorizations. The need to militarily confront a terrorist adversary has, dismayingly, become a permanent fixture of U.S. national security.

Acknowledgments

For their support in thinking through the potential trajectories of the terrorist threat, we thank Bruce Hoffman, Phillip Mudd, Steven Simon, and other attendees at our workshop on the subject. For help understanding the ins and outs of the legal aspects of authorization, we thank the attendees at our workshop on AUMF reform, especially John Bellinger, Rosa Brooks, Benjamin Wittes, and Matthew Waxman. Daniel Silverberg and Robert Karem were extremely helpful in ensuring bipartisan participation in that workshop, as well as in helping us understand the evolving dynamics of the issue in Congress. We are also grateful to the steering committee that helped us get the project off to a solid start and included Admiral Eric Olson, John Bellinger, and Michael Leiter. We benefited much from helpful and constructive reviews by George Jameson, Seth Jones, Adam Grissom, and Benjamin Wittes. Finally, we would like to acknowledge Jack Riley, who saw the pressing need for this work and helped arrange the resources to make it happen.

Abbreviations

AQAP	al Qaeda in the Arabian Peninsula
AQI	al Qaeda in Iraq
AUMF	authorization for the use of military force
DoD	U.S. Department of Defense
H.J. Res.	House joint resolution
ISIL	Islamic State of Iraq and the Levant, also commonly known as the Islamic State of Iraq and Syria (ISIS)
S.J. Res.	Senate joint resolution

Authorities for Military Operations Against Terrorist Groups: The State of the Debate and Options for Congress

Debate over whether or not to reform, revise, or repeal the 2001 and 2002 authorizations for the use of military force (AUMFs) and devise new legislation to combat emerging global terrorist threats has been long-standing.[1] Republicans and Democrats alike have called for Congress to act on some form of the legislation.[2]

The Islamic State of Iraq and the Levant (ISIL) has been responsible for multiple terrorist attacks outside Iraq and Syria, in Lebanon, Egypt, Tunisia, France, Belgium, Turkey, and Jordan, in addition to inspiring violence globally. It claimed credit for and Russia has concluded that ISIL was responsible for the downing of a Russian airliner over Egypt, which killed more than 200 people. And, in Paris, the group organized a series of large-scale attacks that killed more than 130. Officials insisted that France would never buckle to terrorist pressure, and the country launched airstrikes on ISIL's headquarters in Syria. Attacks in Orlando, Florida, and San Bernardino, California, were undertaken in ISIL's name.

---

[1] The 2001 AUMF authorized operations against al Qaeda in response to the 9/11 attacks (Pub. L. 107-40); the 2002 AUMF authorized the war in Iraq (Pub. L. 107-243), which began in 2003. It is important to note that the operations discussed in this report that are permitted under an AUMF include only those under the purview of the Office of the Secretary of Defense. Other activities, such as those conducted by the Intelligence Community (and the Central Intelligence Agency specifically) are authorized through separate processes and congressional notification. Those activities are scrutinized at least as closely as operations under an AUMF, but by different committees using different means.

[2] Leading examples in the move to pass a new authorization are Senator Bob Corker (Republican, Tennessee) and Senator Tim Kaine (Democrat, Virginia).

The United States, too, has ratcheted up its military campaign against ISIL. Limited air assaults have reaped some success, including the destruction of a sizable fleet of fuel trucks and oil production facilities, incinerating large cash stockpiles, facilitating Kurdish advances in both Syria and Iraq, and helping Iraqi forces retake large chunks of territory from ISIL, including Ramadi and, most recently, Fallujah. However, this slow and painstaking progress in the face of aggressive and lethal attacks seems insufficient. Even before the recent spike in attacks, the United States started to put its foot on the gas pedal, promising to increase the frequency and power of airstrikes, sending limited special forces units to Syria to assist with intelligence and targeting, and upping its assistance to the Kurds.

These moves seem sensible in the face of a serious and enduring threat. The need to dismantle ISIL's terrorist and military capacity has gained new urgency. But the shifting battle strategy also presents an opportunity for Congress to weigh in—to add its voice to the calls for a strong response to the growing threat from ISIL. The need for a new AUMF was clear when the air war began; it is now even more important that the newly focused military posture gain a more muscular and tailored legislative underpinning.

Herein, we survey the debate over congressional authorization for counterterrorism operations, describe the terrorist threat to which any such legislation needs to respond and how the military might use force against it, explain what Congress might wish to accomplish with new legislation, offer suggestions on key legislative issues, and consider the implications of different outcomes for U.S. counterterrorism efforts and national security in general.[3]

---

[3]   Important contributions to the debate include Jennifer Daskal and Stephen I. Vladeck, "After the AUMF," *Harvard National Security Journal*, Vol. 5, 2014; Robert Chesney, Jack Goldsmith, Matthew C. Waxman, and Benjamin Wittes, *A Statutory Framework for Next Generation Terrorist Threats*, Hoover Institution, 2013; and Curtis A. Bradley and Jack L. Goldsmith, "Congressional Authorization and the War on Terrorism," *Harvard Law Review*, Vol. 118, No. 7, May 2005. A good deal of important debate on the question has occurred on the website Lawfareblog.com, which contains a plethora of well-informed commentary and perspectives on AUMF reform.

Our approach to the research was threefold. First, we consulted with a small group of former senior national security officials to help guide the effort and to advise on our approach. They helped us define the research task, illuminate controversies, and provide context for the analysis presented here—for example, clarifying that the lack of a new AUMF would likely not have a significant operational impact. Second, we conducted a comprehensive literature review to identify the issues and positions pertaining to the AUMF debate. Third, we held two workshops with top experts on the global terrorism threat and the AUMF legal framework. In the first workshop, which focused on the terrorism threat, we asked four experts to present their perspectives on the terrorist landscape and how it might develop in the next five years. We benchmarked the current threat environment and then explored three alternative future trajectories: a best case, a worst case, and a wildcard scenario. This exercise formed the basis of our understanding of relationships among the key terrorist actors and the enduring need for a counterterrorism AUMF. The second workshop focused on specific elements of that AUMF. We invited prominent and respected experts representing a diversity of views for a bipartisan discussion of the issue. They helped clarify the arguments behind the strongly held views on both sides of the AUMF debate, with one side seeking maximum flexibility for the President to prosecute the military's counterterrorism mission and the other favoring restrictions and limitations. In surveying the current thinking among experts, we were able to gauge the spectrum of views on the subject, ascertain the most important elements of an AUMF, and, with the addition of insights on counterterrorism operations and the threat trajectory, develop suggestions for Congress.

Our bottom line is that although existing authorization can and has been made to work against a range of extremist groups, it still needs to be updated, if only because the threat has changed dramatically since the initial legislation was passed. A new authorization that more clearly targets the current threat is preferable and would signal clear and renewed U.S. resolve to combat terrorism.

Indeed, the central question in any authorization process is less about whether the President can, in practice, use force against terrorist groups than whether Congress is willing to support these operations. Failing to do so could appear to many to abrogate an important congressional responsibility implicit in the Constitution and undercut the United States' international credibility.

There is still a need for military operations against the diminished (but by no means defeated) al Qaeda core organization and its associates.[4] Hence, any attempt to rescind the original 2001 authorization without passing new laws would be a dangerous strategic miscalculation. While significant progress has been made in degrading the group that attacked the United States on 9/11, a new AUMF would offer an opportunity to clarify that the danger from that group and groups associated with it (such as al Qaeda in the Arabian Peninsula [AQAP] and the Nusrah Front) persists.[5] But, if the goal of a new AUMF is to adapt to the changed threat environment, new legislation should also cover new groups.

Congress might also consider identifying a clear purpose for counterterrorism operations, authorizing the broadest possible range of military operations against ISIL and associated groups, imposing adequate reporting requirements, and including a reasonable renewal term.

Ground force restrictions, such as those included in the White House's 2015 proposed authorization are, as a general principle, undesirable. That said, the language the White House proposed was not limiting in any meaningful sense and would not, in practical terms, constrain strategic options in the near term, when the main constraint will continue to be widespread public reticence about repeating the experience of the past 12 years in Iraq.[6]

---

[4] Seth G. Jones, *A Persistent Threat: The Evolution of al Qa'ida and Other Salafi Jihadists*, Santa Monica, Calif.: RAND Corporation, RR-637-OSD, 2014.

[5] See Jones, 2014.

[6] Despite broader support for general military operations in these areas, only 39 percent of those polled by the Pew Research Center in October 2014 favored sending U.S. ground forces into Iraq and Syria, whereas 55 percent were opposed. See Pew Research Center, "Support for U.S. Campaign Against ISIS; Doubts About Its Effectiveness, Objectives," October 2014.

Again, AUMF reform would mainly provide a strong statement of congressional and broader public support for U.S. military operations against an evolving terrorist threat, especially, but not exclusively, from ISIL.

Why Use Force?

The United States faces a challenge from terrorist groups that it will have to grapple with for many years to come. This challenge stems from deeper changes in the nature of the international system that allow even small groups of ideological fanatics to threaten significant numbers of innocent people with terrorist attacks. Although individual groups can be dismantled, the phenomenon altogether cannot be vanquished in the same way as a traditional state-based threat. The degree of risk these groups create for U.S. security, however, can certainly be managed and significantly reduced through the use of U.S. military force alongside other tools of U.S. power.

An effective strategy against terrorist threats is multifaceted and includes diplomatic, political, financial, law enforcement, intelligence, and military tools, used in concert to reduce the threat posed by terrorist groups that would target the United States, its allies, and global interests. Military force is an important component of this approach. The record shows that the use of force against terrorist groups, in general, has been beneficial. Since 9/11, the number of terrorist attacks globally may have increased, but many attacks that would have occurred against the United States have been thwarted.[7] In 2001, the United States faced a concerted, well-funded terrorist organization with global reach: al Qaeda. Al Qaeda would surely have succeeded in other potentially 9/11-like attacks against the United States if the United States had abjured the use of military force in its overall counterterrorism strategy.

---

[7] Lauren B. O'Brien, "The Evolution of Terrorism Since 9/11," *FBI Law Enforcement Bulletin*, September 2011.

This is not to argue or draw conclusions about whether the counterterrorism strategy of the United States and its allies has been optimal, which is a separate question. Nor is it to argue that the use of force has no downsides, much less that force is the appropriate response to all counterterrorism challenges. Rather, a reasonable set of assumptions about what would have happened if the United States had not used force against al Qaeda leads to the conclusion that force was just one critical element of an effective U.S. response. Improved homeland defense, like many other aspects of the national counterterrorism strategy, was critical to reducing the terrorist threat to the United States and other countries, but the use of military power offensively and overseas was equally important and will remain so.

There is moreover plenty of evidence that leaving terrorist groups alone is a risky strategy. This is what happened in Afghanistan in the 1990s, where al Qaeda was permitted safe haven and subsequently grew into a global menace that took thousands of American lives. Similarly, in Iraq and Syria after the Arab Spring, ISIL benefited from a permissive environment to achieve unprecedented gains and go further than even al Qaeda in establishing a caliphate whose objective is the destruction of the United States and its allies.

The U.S. military (like other militaries) uses force to combat terrorist organizations overseas in multiple ways. On the most basic level, counterterrorism operations deplete enemy ranks by capturing or killing terrorist fighters. The vast majority of these operations are high-precision strikes conducted by special forces ground teams or air-ground attack aircraft, such as armed drones, with the aim of capturing or killing high-value targets. (Although AUMFs cover only Title 10 U.S. Department of Defense [DoD] operations,[8] the operational objectives are the same for Title 10 operations carried out by non-DoD U.S. government entities under Title 50 authority.)

---

[8] The authorities conveyed under Title 10 and Title 50 are too complicated and intricate to detail here. For our purposes, we define the distinction as between those authorities that provide the legal basis for the roles, missions, and organization of the branches of the armed services and DoD under Title 10 of the U.S. Code and those authorities that do the same for the Intelligence Community under Title 50 of the U.S. Code.

In rare cases, military force may be used on a larger scale against terrorist groups that opt to fight conventionally and thus present a larger target. This was the case, for example, with French operations against al Qaeda in the Islamic Maghreb in Mali in January 2013. Most operations aimed at depleting enemy ranks target specific high-value targets, however. Usually, these targets are leaders of terrorist groups, and the strikes aim to decapitate the group. Decapitation strikes are sometimes controversial (particularly when used against Americans, like Anwar Awlaki), but they can be very effective tools in dismantling terrorist networks because most terrorist organizations are held together by a select few, often charismatic leaders. Eliminating these individuals can significantly reduce the unity of the group, creating internal strife about leadership succession, and depriving the group of important managerial skill sets, connections, and other assets it needs to sustain its networks, maintain continuity of operations, and survive.

To be sure, there is some debate about the effectiveness of decapitation strikes, but most experts agree that under certain conditions they can be an important way to deal a major blow to terrorist groups. Leading examples include the successful targeting of Abu Musab al Zarqawi and Osama Bin Laden, which weakened (but did not necessarily defeat) al Qaeda in Iraq (AQI) and al Qaeda's core, respectively. Hundreds of strikes against al Qaeda over the past 14 years have certainly not defeated the ideology, but they have weakened the organization and thereby greatly reduced the threat.

Beyond killing individuals, military force, along with the threat of military force, impedes the operations of terrorist groups. Combined with other efforts, military force can complicate a terrorist group's recruitment, financing, logistics, and other activities by forcing terrorists to operate under extreme secrecy and making would-be recruits and supporters risk death to participate. In other words, by deterring some individuals and groups from supporting and associating with the terrorist group, the threat of military force can complicate terrorist operations. Deterrence by threat of violence is unlikely to have much impact on zealots like Osama Bin Laden, but it can have a significant impact on the individuals and groups that sustain these organizations—in other words, the network on which terrorist groups rely.[9]

By deterring cooperation among terrorist groups and reducing recruitment, military operations also reduce terrorist mobility, forcing terrorists to operate under adverse conditions that thereby hamper their effectiveness. The threat of military strikes is one way to force terrorist groups to take precautionary measures, to travel carefully, and to operate clandestinely. Clandestine operations are costly and incur risks. As recent scholarship has demonstrated, these costs can include a diminution in command and control along with financial and other costs.[10] Targeting these mechanisms is key to reducing the tempo of terrorist groups. If terrorist groups are forced to divert resources to maintain their security and question whether it is safe for them to move around, they will spend less time plotting and launching attacks. A concerted military campaign provides an additional benefit in making the groups question their own security and the loyalty of their ranks.

Groups can be forced to operate under adverse conditions by military pressure under different circumstances, but the most important is when military operations target a terrorist safe haven. Safe havens are areas where terrorist groups are able to operate with impunity, often controlling some or all of the local governance structures. Examples include parts of Afghanistan prior to 2001, parts of Somalia and Nigeria in recent years, Northern Mali in 2012, and parts of Libya, Yemen, and Iraq today. Safe havens allow terrorist organizations to plan, recruit, train, and build ties to other terrorist individuals and groups, making them veritable factories for violent radicalism.

Finally, military tools are used both directly and indirectly to strengthen partners in their own efforts to combat terrorism so that these governments can, themselves, defeat terrorist organizations operating in their territory or region. In many cases, the most appropriate vector for preventive or coercive action against terrorist groups are the

---

[9]   See Matthew H. Kroenig and Barry Pavel, "How to Deter Terrorism," *Washington Quarterly*, Spring 2012.

[10] Jacob N. Shapiro, *The Terrorist's Dilemma: Managing Violent Covert Organizations*, Princeton, N.J.: Princeton University Press, 2013.

military and defense establishments of the countries where the terrorist groups operate. Training and equipping military forces in Africa, the Middle East, South Asia, Latin America, and elsewhere to effectively target terrorist groups while supporting governance reform is one of the most promising military counterterrorism strategies available.[11]

As part of these partnering operations, the U.S. military may be called to perform a much broader range of tasks than in cases that involve targeting individual terrorists in a straightforward way. Additional tasks, beyond training and equipping partner forces, may include strategic communication, providing logistical or other support to forces being trained, providing support for development projects, and guiding institutional reforms. Some of these tasks do not involve the use of military force, per se, but they are worth noting as a reminder of the breadth of tasks in which the military might become involved in a given counterterrorism effort.

In short, the military is called upon to conduct a broad range of operations to combat terrorist groups. These require multiple different subordinate military operations and tactics, ranging from intelligence collection to ground force deployments, air strikes, supply and logistics, training capability, and more.

An Evolving and Unpredictable Threat

The terrorist threat has morphed considerably since the attacks on September 11, 2001.[12] The overriding concern then was with Osama Bin Laden and his relatively small gang of disciplined, committed terrorists whose principal target was the U.S. homeland. That small group—now referred to as "core" al Qaeda—remains dangerous, but the threat of

---

[11] RAND research has addressed this topic extensively. For an overview of efforts to build partner security capacity, see, for example, Christopher Paul, Colin P. Clarke, Beth Grill, Stephanie Young, Jennifer D. P. Moroney, Joe Hogler, and Christine Leah, *What Works Best When Building Partner Capacity and Under What Circumstances?* Santa Monica, Calif.: RAND Corporation, MG-1253/1-OSD, 2013.

[12] This section benefits from discussions at a workshop held at RAND on November 12, 2014, with Bruce Hoffman, Steven Simon, Philip Mudd, Seth Jones, and others.

another spectacular attack against the West has receded. In its place, however, a new threat, more fragmented and diffuse, has emerged. That threat is made both more dangerous and more complicated by the emergence of ISIL and its control of a large swath of territory in Iraq and Syria.[13]

In 2001, al Qaeda was a relatively poorly understood group, but it had just launched the most successful terrorist attack in history. It was based in South Asia—specifically, in Afghanistan—yet its shadowy tentacles reached into Africa, Southeast Asia, and Europe. The basis for the U.S. threat assessment then was threefold: the preeminence of the United States as a threat and target, Bin Laden's cohesive leadership of the global jihadist movement, and the likelihood of follow-on attacks similar to those launched on 9/11, which appeared high.

ISIL arguably emanates from a similar ideological basis as al Qaeda, but it stretches credulity to argue that it is allied with al Qaeda or an associated force. The bitter feud between the two leaders, Ayman al-Zawahiri and Abu Bakr al-Baghdadi, that led to ISIL's purge from the official al Qaeda organization, as well as bitter and bloody battles between the two in Syria, have demonstrated how far apart the two organizations have grown. Some elements of the two groups may cooperate at tactical levels in the fight against the Assad regime in Syria and against Shia and Kurdish forces in Iraq, but they are fundamentally at odds. Indeed, rather than cooperate or join forces, it is more likely that al Qaeda and ISIL will compete for recruits, resources, and territory.[14]

Even before the emergence of ISIL, the threat that national security experts envisaged on the eve of 9/11 had evolved very differently than anticipated. In the nearly 15 years since 9/11, al Qaeda has changed significantly from its original core of globally focused jihadists, which is now diminished, to encompass affiliates in Somalia, Yemen, Iraq, and North Africa, which pose new threats and opened new geographic opportunities for global jihad.

---

[13] Aaron Y. Zelin, *The Islamic State: A Video Introduction*, Washington, D.C.: Washington Institute for Near East Policy, January 13, 2015.

[14] Daniel Byman and Jennifer Williams, "ISIS vs. Al Qaeda: Jihadism's Global Civil War," *National Interest*, February 24, 2015.

If the twists and turns of the evolution of al Qaeda posed both new challenges and redefined the nature of the threat, the emergence of ISIL dramatically shifted priorities and, importantly, changed the strategies required to combat the threat. The group's quick sweep through eastern Syria and western Iraq put U.S. partners at risk, menaced the Shia government in Baghdad, and offered a large new safe haven for dangerous global terrorists.

Dismantling core al Qaeda in Pakistan was an important milestone against global terrorism. The original group that attacked the United States on 9/11 has been significantly degraded, but America still faces serious threats. Some experts argue that the threat from terrorism has not receded but instead has worsened. Rather than centered on one predominant group—al Qaeda core—the threat has become dispersed, both ideologically and geographically.[15] Instead of one hierarchical group with one identifiable leader and a coherent ideology, the United States now faces a multitude of groups with diverse priorities. Geographically, the reach of terrorist groups and their choice of safe havens have expanded from Afghanistan (before 9/11) to Iraq, Syria, Yemen, Somalia, Libya, Nigeria, and much of the Sahel now. Terrorists have expanded in terms of sheer numbers and recruiting, as evidenced by the massive foreign influx of volunteers to ISIL and in terms of influence as well. Pro-ISIL and other groups in the Sinai, Boko Haram in Nigeria, and multiple groups in Libya and Tunisia are bound ideologically, if not organizationally, to Bin Laden's core messages. Their sophisticated use of social media and their reach into the West have improved dramatically.

This complex and evolving threat, while increasingly challenging to understand and combat, poses a different kind of problem for the United States. Attacks in Somalia against regional forces and civilians, the ominous presence and potential of AQAP in Yemen in the context of that country's collapsed political fabric, and the continued presence (despite the successful French intervention) of al Qaeda–linked forces in the Sahel all pose challenges and potential threats. As a previous RAND work has enumerated, success against al Qaeda core has in no

---

[15] Jones, 2014.

way diminished (and indeed may have exacerbated) the threat from jihadist organizations.[16] The global jihad is no longer dominated by one group but is now characterized by competition and infighting between al Qaeda and ISIL.

This atomization of the threat, along with the rise of so many new groups and alliances, has made estimating the threat trajectory a difficult and uncertain task. Where the United States might once have hoped for the eventual demise of core al Qaeda in the wake of major leadership losses, such as Bin Laden's death, so many different actors evolving on independent axes significantly increases the unpredictability of the future threat and decreases the accuracy of future threat projections. This creates a significant problem for Congress when it comes to specifying the threat against which military force is authorized.

To complicate the decisionmaking calculus further, in addition to growing more diverse, the focus of many terrorist adversaries has shifted since 9/11 from a near obsession with attacking the West ("the far enemy") to more local priorities and politics. The spread of militancy has been accompanied by a localization of the fight. Al Qaeda certainly still brandishes the global jihad, and recent attacks in Paris, Ottawa, and Sydney are sufficient evidence that the threat persists globally.[17] But new groups and even al Qaeda affiliates are becoming more involved in local battles and appear to be dedicating fewer resources to global targets.

Many threats cause local calamity but pose limited threats to the West. Dozens of groups in the Muslim world destabilize regional governments and terrorize local residents but pose only marginal risk beyond their immediate environs. Boko Haram in Nigeria drew worldwide media attention when it kidnapped hundreds of local schoolgirls. It has been responsible for countless civilian deaths and is a menace

---

[16] Jones, 2014.

[17] In January 2015, attackers who claimed to be motivated by either AQAP or ISIL killed 17 people in a series of attacks in Paris, including at the offices of the satirical magazine *Charlie Hebdo*. In October 2014, a single shooter killed a Canadian soldier and fired shots inside one of the Canadian Parliament's buildings. In December 2014, an armed attacker with unknown motives held several customers and employees hostage at a Lindt chocolate shop in Sydney.

to Nigeria's population. But, even after announcing its union with ISIL, it has not displayed either the intent or the capacity to attack the U.S. homeland. Many other groups, including Ansar al Dine and various factions of Ansar al Sharia, are locally poisonous but have limited broader reach. While the United States may wish to use military force against such groups, the appropriate strategy is not the same as for ISIL.

The threat is also dynamic, has developed unevenly, and can be quite unpredictable. It is dynamic because as some existing groups lose capacity (mostly due to effective counterterrorism operations), others emerge.[18] The al Qaeda core is still a threat, but one that is secondary to its own affiliate in Yemen—as it attested when it attempted three aviation attacks against the United States, something core al Qaeda has not pulled off. It is uneven because not all "militant jihadist groups" pose similar threats. It is no longer as simple as it was on the eve of 9/11, when Bin Laden ruled the global jihad and his followers agreed to the straightforward thesis that the West (specifically, the United States) was its primary enemy and attacks must be focused on that target.[19] Many of the groups that Bin Laden's ideology has spawned, from Boko Haram in Nigeria to a wide variety of groups in North Africa and even al Shabaab in Somalia, are intensely anti-Western but have focused most of their terrorism against local targets.

In these conditions, one of the most significant challenges from a counterterrorism perspective is to assess and identify which groups are likely to shift from being largely local concerns to being potential threats to the United States and U.S. homeland. The unpredictable volubility of the threat poses a serious problem when it comes to congressional authorization for the use of military force, simply because the groups against which force is being authorized are subject to rapid change in capabilities and even intentions.

---

[18] Matthew G. Olsen, director, National Counterterrorism Center, statement before the Committee on Homeland Security, U.S. House of Representatives, at the hearing "Worldwide Threats to the Homeland," September 17, 2014.

[19] Nicholas J. Rasmussen, director, National Counterterrorism Center, statement before the Select Committee on Intelligence, U.S. Senate, at the hearing "Current Terrorist Threat to the United States," February 12, 2015.

The unsettling truth is that the difference between a plot to attack a local mall in Kenya, for example, and a mall in Europe or the United States may be as simple as the availability of an operative with the right profile and passport. If one believes its rhetoric, al Nusrah in Syria (and, especially, the embedded Khorasan group) has a very specific anti-Western agenda. Al Qaeda affiliates reportedly intend to attack Western targets; AQAP has repeatedly tried and seems intent to continue to try to launch such operations. Al Shabaab has never toned down its virulent anti-Western message, and al Qaeda in the Islamic Maghreb propaganda has been both anti-French and anti-Western. The fact that few of these organizations have attempted attacks in the United States has more to do with good defenses, long distances, and difficulty in accessing targets with capable operatives.[20]

A principal challenge for Congress is to craft an authorization for operations against both the old, persistent threat (al Qaeda and its affiliates and other groups ideologically aligned with the broader jihadist movement) and the new, emerging threat (ISIL and its allies). Al Qaeda and its ilk have not gone away; they continue to orchestrate credible threats to Europe, the United States, and elsewhere in the West. The experts in Yemen who designed the explosives, trained the operatives, and launched repeated attempted attacks against Western-bound aviation are still at large and remain intent on attacking the West.

It is important not to overestimate the ability to describe the taxonomy of terrorist enemies, however. For example, AQAP in Yemen appears to be loyal to the al Qaeda core, for now. Indeed, its chief is Zawahiri's deputy for the organization. But more voices, particularly as the Shia upstart Houthis control the Yemeni capital, are speaking in more favorable terms about ISIL and are critical of how al Qaeda has responded to this new threat.

Any authorization that Congress drafts should focus on the full range of potential directions in which the terrorist threat could go. This is a broad and frightening range. Although one would hope that the global terrorist threat will diminish—and it might—the more

---

[20] National Counterterrorism Center, "Al Qa'ida in the Arabian Peninsula (AQAP)," *Counterterrorism Guide*, undated(a).

ISIL: A Different Kind of Terrorist Adversary

ISIL is different from other terrorist groups. Other terrorist groups have controlled territory and attempted to govern, but none have so quickly sought legitimacy by declaring a state—in this case, a caliphate. Unlike other jihadist organizations, particularly al Qaeda, ISIL is open about its aims, its recruitment, and its propaganda. It is different in this way from the typical terrorist organizations, which have operated mostly in the shadows and attempted to avoid public scrutiny.

ISIL's grab for territory has some precedents, yet none so brazen or successful. Salafi-jihadist groups have often run into trouble governing territory, as demonstrated by al Shabaab in Somalia and AQAP in Yemen. In many ways, ISIL is different from all other terrorist threats that the United States has previously faced, largely because it is more than just a terrorist group. No other terrorist group has carved out so much territory, claimed statehood and legitimacy, established such a wide-ranging propaganda machine, or attracted so much attention so quickly.

ISIL's successful occupation of a large swath of Syria and Iraq and its continued tactical success even in the face of recent Kurdish, Syrian, and Iraqi resistance and U.S.-led airstrikes suggest a resilience that will take some time to reverse. The group is very different from al Qaeda, and it poses a very different threat. It clearly represents a more immediate danger to U.S. allies in the region, including the Kurds, minorities in Syria and Iraq, and the government of Iraq itself. It is also a direct threat to U.S. interests in the region and an indirect threat to the homeland (insofar as it has motivated specific threats and broadly encouraged attacks against Americans, both domestically and abroad). In contrast, elements within al Qaeda probably remain more acute transnational threats, with a clear intent and capability to launch attacks more akin to the al Qaeda of old (against aviation, transportation, and other soft targets).

Any reversals will depend on the success of coalition airpower and the ground forces of an untested and retrained Iraqi army and Shia militias; an ill-defined and divided Syrian opposition; outnumbered Syrian regime forces supported by Iran, Russia, and Hezbollah; and overstretched Kurdish fighters. In a matter of months, ISIL has become the most immediate threat to the Middle East.

ISIL is a militia, an army, and even a nascent government with structures and ministries—and it both promotes violence among its supporters and has terrorists embedded within it. Thus, the United States is not waging just counterterrorism operations; it is also waging a serious and long-term counterinsurgency effort that is more akin to conventional war than it is to counterterrorism. It is not simply targeting small cells that are plotting attacks or the leadership of a relatively isolated terrorist group. In this regard, ISIL may demand not just a counterterrorism operation but also a conventional (and likely long-term) military operation stretching across multiple continents.

SOURCES: National Counterterrorism Center, "Islamic State of Iraq and the Levant (ISIL)," *Counterterrorism Guide*, undated(b); Zachary Laub and Jonathan Masters, *The Islamic State*, backgrounder, New York: Council on Foreign Relations, May 18, 2015; Michael Weiss and Hassan Hassan, *Inside the Army of Terror*, New York: Reagan Arts, 2015.

likely scenario is that it will be at least as much a concern in five years as it is today. In a worst-case scenario, ISIL could establish a semi-permanent base in Syria and Iraq and use it to attack and expand much farther. Al Qaeda could succeed in expanding in India or reestablishing a foothold in Afghanistan. AQAP could solidify a safe haven in Yemen from which to plot attacks against the United States. ISIL, al Nusrah's Khorasan group, or even core al Qaeda could also manage successful attacks in Europe and or the United States, akin to or worse than the January and November 2015 attacks in Paris.

These are not happy prospects, but they are realities that should be considered.

A Changing Debate

The legislation under which the U.S. military conducts counter-terrorism operations worldwide against al Qaeda dates from 2001. Written only a few weeks after the 9/11 attacks, the 2001 AUMF provides the executive branch with broad authorization to conduct military operations against the perpetrators of those attacks and their associates for the purposes of defending the United States against future attacks by these groups. Specifically, it authorizes the President to use

> all necessary and appropriate force against those nations, organizations, or persons he determines planned, authorized, committed, or aided the terrorist attacks that occurred on September 11, 2001, or harbored such organizations or persons, in order to prevent any future acts of international terrorism against the United States.[21]

In addition to the 2001 authorization, Congress authorized the Iraq War in 2002. Although conceived when the United States was preparing for the invasion that would ultimately bring down Saddam

---

[21] Public Law 107-40, 2001, Sec. 2(a). See also Barack Obama, "Joint Resolution to Authorize the Limited Use of the United States Armed Forces Against the Islamic State of Iraq and the Levant," draft authorization, February 11, 2015.

Hussein, that legislation has resurfaced as an important part of the debate in the wake of ISIL's capture of a large part of Iraqi territory.[22]

Overall, the terrorist threat has changed significantly since 9/11, raising the question of whether or not the 2001 authorization has outlived its time and whether new legislation is needed that more accurately addresses the challenge described in the preceding section. From a strictly legal perspective, a case can be and has been made that ISIL is sufficiently close to al Qaeda, at least ideologically, that it can be construed to be covered under the 2001 AUMF. Nevertheless, the two organizations are at war with each other, fighting for adherents and leadership of the global Jihadist movement, and are engaged in bloody combat in Syria and Iraq. Although they have common roots, the fact that they are currently killing each other's forces argues that ISIL is sufficiently distinct from al Qaeda to warrant a separate authorization.

Calls for reform have come from different perspectives.[23] We focus in this report on the debate between those who advocate a broad authorization with few limits and those who prefer a narrower remit with more restrictions. We acknowledge that there are also those who argue that the whole debate is wrongheaded, that the real question is not under what circumstances the President is allowed to use force but whether force should be used at all. We do not take up that set of arguments here, however.

Debate over AUMF reform was kindled in part by a 2013 paper published by the Hoover Institution in which a set of top legal experts argued that the 2001 authorization should be replaced because it no

---

[22] Public Law 107-243, 2002.

[23] The two prominent schools of thought are represented, broadly, by arguments by those who seek to give the President a free hand in combating terrorists and those who seek to limit the President's powers. See David Cohen, "John McCain: Don't Handcuff President," *Politico*, February 15, 2015, and Benjamin Wittes, senior fellow, Brookings Institution, statement before the Committee on Armed Forces, U.S. House of Representatives, at the hearing "Outside Perspectives on the President's Proposed Authorization for the Use of Military Force Against the Islamic State of Iraq and the Levant," February 26, 2015. Senator Tim Kaine has often expressed his views on limiting ground forces, see "In AUMF Hearing, Kaine Renews Call for Swift, Bipartisan Congressional Action and Presses for Clarity on Ground Troops," press release, March 11, 2015.

longer accurately reflected the threat the nation faced.[24] This is a sound rationale for reform, as we discuss later, but it is only one of the issues dividing camps in the debate.

The paper's authors laid out several options for updating the 2001 legislation, all of which aimed to preserve the legislation's broad authority for military operations while updating the groups that were associated with it. Their favored approach was that Congress provide broad authorization for military operations against a list of terrorist organizations that would be updated on a regular basis according to the current threat they posed. The authors favored congressional action but with no new limitations on the actual use of force and the possible enlargement of the groups against which force might be used.

Several legal experts have criticized this position on the grounds that while new authorization is needed, it should be more restrictive due to the progress made since 2001 in dismantling al Qaeda. These experts also claim that the 2001 authorization has permitted a never-ending, even self-perpetuating war. For example, two leading experts favoring reform warned that calls for such legislation "perpetuate war at a time when we should be seeking to end it."[25] The *New York Times* editorial board similarly argued that the 2001 authorization had "warped into . . . the basis for a vast overreaching of power by one president, Mr. Bush, and less outrageous but still dangerous policies by another, Barack Obama."[26] This camp has argued not only that the authorization enables a "forever war," but it has also argued that the authorization's use far outstrips the original objectives of Congress.[27] Some key members of Congress involved in drafting the 2001 legislation have also stepped in to support this view.[28] These experts warn

---

[24] Chesney et al., 2013, p. 3.

[25] Daskal and Vladeck, 2014, p. 119.

[26] "Repeal the Military Force Law," *New York Times*, March 9, 2013.

[27] See, for example, Bill French and John Bradshaw, *Ending the Endless War*, Washington, D.C.: National Security Network, August 2014.

[28] See, for example, Tom Daschle, "Power We Didn't Grant," *Washington Post*, December 23, 2005; Glenn Greenwald, "Barbara Lee and Dick Durbin's 'Nobody-Could-Have-Known' Defense," *The Guardian*, May 7, 2013.

that the American public has little knowledge of which groups can be considered "associated forces" of al Qaeda and thus be targeted by the U.S. military.[29]

Arguments in favor of more restrictive legislation gained ground after Bin Laden was killed in the 2011 Abbottabad operation. In 2012 and 2013, the Obama administration seemed to favor this view. In a speech at the National Defense University in May 2013, the President said he would seek reform of the 2001 authorization on the grounds that "all wars must end."[30] Similarly, DoD legal counsel Jeh Johnson said in a November 2012 speech at the Oxford Union, "'War' must be regarded as a finite, extraordinary and unnatural state of affairs."[31] This view put the White House in the somewhat unusual position of requesting that Congress vote to limit its powers to conduct military operations.

In 2014, however, the addition of ISIL to the mix significantly changed the outlook. As a radical, new organization, ISIL's emergence underscored the inherent problem with basing anti-ISIL operations on the 2001 AUMF, which focused on al Qaeda, while at the same time greatly weakening the argument that the global terrorist threat was winding down as a result of al Qaeda's decline. This was a significant shift in the debate that underscored the need for reform, but it took the discussion in a new direction that many had not predicted.

Over the course of the fall of 2014, the White House changed course from its earlier statements that appeared to favor a more restrictive authorization. Initially, the White House had indicated that it believed it had the authorities necessary for operations against ISIL. It argued, in particular, that a combination of authority from the 2001 AUMF, the 2002 AUMF that authorized the war in Iraq, and the President's prerogatives under Article II of the Constitution was sufficient for coalition operations in Iraq and Syria. Nevertheless, it remained the

---

[29] Daskal and Vladeck, 2014, p. 124.

[30] White House, "Remarks by the President at the National Defense University," transcript, May 23, 2013.

[31] David Ingram, "U.S. War on al Qaeda Is Not Indefinite—Pentagon Lawyer," Reuters, December 1, 2012.

administration's preference to revise the 2001 AUMF, repeal the 2002 Iraq AUMF, and draft a new authorization against ISIL.[32]

An important aspect of the administration's argument that cast ISIL as an "associated force" of al Qaeda was that some members of ISIL had once been members of al Qaeda in Iraq. They also pointed out that individuals in other terror groups had acknowledged ISIL as the true inheritor of Bin Laden's legacy. It is also clear that ISIL is attempting to become the successor to al Qaeda in leading the global jihad.[33] In October 2014, National Counterterrorism Center director Matthew Olsen said that ISIL "started as [al Qaeda in Iraq]. . . . They've sort of maintained the same hierarchy, some of the same goals, some of the same tactics in terms of levels of violence. . . . They maintain that they are the true inheritors of bin Laden's legacy."[34]

It is true that ISIL was linked historically to al Qaeda in Iraq, but ISIL later renounced its membership in al Qaeda. Considering it an associated force under the 2001 authorization was therefore something of a legal stretch. Tactical alliances and some limited cooperation on the ground notwithstanding, the split between al Qaeda and ISIL is more than an argument between two factions representing similar ideologies. It is basic, deeply rooted, and likely permanent. As discussed later in this report, these differences extend to a fundamental schism about goals: Al Qaeda, rooted in the ideology of Bin Laden, bases its vision on the distant future, targeting the "far enemy" first to eliminate its presence in the region, followed by the defeat of apostate regimes from Morocco to South Asia and the eventual realization of an Islamic caliphate. In stark contrast, ISIL evinces no such patience, and its premature (at least in the eyes of al Qaeda's more traditional jihadists)

---

[32] John Kerry, Secretary of State, statement before the Committee on Foreign Relations, U.S. Senate, at the hearing "Authorization to Use Force Against ISIL," December 9, 2014.

[33] J. M. Berger, "The Islamic State vs. al Qaeda," *Foreign Policy*, September 2, 2014.

[34] "Views from Washington: The Changing Terrorist Threat," video of discussion with Matthew Olsen at Harvard Law School, October 8, 2014.

establishment of a caliphate and the imposition of harsh sharia law and penalties underscores this different approach.[35]

For these reasons, the 2002 AUMF does not convincingly apply to operations against ISIL. The 2002 AUMF was conceived to authorize force against Saddam Hussein's regime—a traditional state, not a nonstate actor. In justifying the legality of its operations against ISIL, the administration seemed on weak ground on at least two of three fronts. Presidential authorities under Article II of the Constitution are less debatable but a potentially undesirable basis on which to base the argument, as discussed later.

The White House appears to have been sensitive to the fragility of its position and changed course in late 2014. The President stated on November 4, 2014, that he would, in fact, seek authorization from Congress, despite having argued that it was not necessary, strictly speaking.[36] In other words, while the White House preferred to have Congress authorize its operations in Iraq and Syria, it did not think congressional authorization was *required* for those operations. (This position was likely reinforced by an abortive effort a year earlier to obtain congressional authorization for strikes against the Assad regime after it used chemical weapons against civilian populations.)

In December 2014, Secretary of State John Kerry testified on the subject before the Senate Foreign Relations Committee. It was a lame-duck Congress, but the testimony was a preview of the authorization that the administration would request the following February. Kerry outlined two key points: The authorization would give the President "a clear mandate and flexibility" to conduct military operations, but it would be "limited and specific to the threat posed."[37] What this meant, Kerry went on to explain, was an authorization focused on ISIL anywhere in the world; it also ruled out the use of ground forces and required renewal after three years. A bill based on this recommenda-

---

[35] Aaron Y. Zelin, "Al-Qaeda Disaffiliates with the Islamic State of Iraq and al-Sham," policy alert, Washington, D.C.: Washington Institute, February 4, 2014.

[36] Molly O'Toole, "Obama to Ask Congress for New War Powers to Fight ISIS," *Defense One*, November 5, 2014.

[37] Kerry, 2014.

tion passed the Senate committee shortly after Kerry's testimony, but the passage was only symbolic, given that the Republicans were poised to retake Congress in January.

On February 11, 2015, the President addressed the topic again in a letter to Congress, accompanied by proposed authorization text.[38] The draft requested authority for operations specifically against ISIL and "associated persons or forces" without geographic limitation and with a three-year renewal term. The White House draft also ruled out "enduring offensive ground combat operations," a clause that was sure to provoke partisan debate.

Indeed, one of the most curious aspects of the White House draft was that it did not address the original 2001 legislation and, in this regard, appeared to be an about face. Not only had previous statements from the White House favored reforming the 2001 legislation, by not addressing the existing 2001 legislation, the White House made the debate less relevant than it might have been.[39] In his letter to Congress accompanying the February draft text, the President stated his commitment to "working with the Congress and the American people to refine, and ultimately repeal, the 2001 AUMF," but the draft AUMF itself neither rescinded nor superseded the 2001 legislation. Indeed, it rescinded the *2002* AUMF, a relatively uncontroversial move. It thus clearly did not take any steps to end what many administration supporters called "the forever war" in Iraq. To the contrary, its effect was to significantly broaden the authorization for that war.[40]

The Purpose and Role of Congressional Authorization

Superficially, the language and tenor of the debate over authorizations could lead one to conclude that congressional authorizations actually directly circumscribe what the executive branch, and, thus, the

---

[38] Obama, 2015.

[39] Jack Goldsmith, "The Administration's Hard-to-Fathom Draft AUMF," *Lawfare Blog*, February 12, 2015.

[40] Obama, 2015.

U.S. military, are able to do. This is not the case. Understanding what authorizations do and do not do, and the purpose they actually serve, is critical to assessing what they ought and ought not to include.

To begin with, congressional authorizations are not as important to military operations as one might think. Constitutional experts agree that the President already has the authority to conduct military operations in defense of the nation under Article II of the Constitution.[41] Historically, there has been extensive debate about how far that presidential authority can be taken, specifically with regard to the ability to preempt threats and how imminent a threat must be before Article II authority is invoked. The War Powers Resolution of 1973 requires the executive branch to ask for congressional authorization after 60 days of hostilities (with another 30 days to complete a withdrawal if no authorization is provided), but few administrations have actually complied with this statute when using military force (though they have normally reported to Congress). In a crisis situation that threatened an important U.S. interest, it is nearly unthinkable that a President would choose not to take military action to defend the nation solely because Congress had not authorized it.

If most scholars agree that the President already has the authority to carry out military operations absent congressional authorization, why should the President seek congressional approval?

One reason is to maintain good relations with Congress. During the 2011 Libya operation, the White House damaged its support on both sides of the aisle when it ultimately opted not to seek congressional authorization.[42] The oversight resulted in resolutions sponsored by both Democrats and Republicans ordering the administration to cease operations. The congressional response included resolutions introduced by Democratic Senator Jim Webb of Virginia on one side of the partisan debate and by Republican Senator Bob Corker of Tennessee on the other demanding that the President seek Senate and House approval before continuing the mission.

---

[41] See, especially, Daskal and Vladeck, 2014, and Bradley and Goldsmith, 2005.

[42] See Christopher S. Chivvis, *Toppling Qaddafi: Libya and the Limits of Liberal Intervention*, New York: Cambridge University Press, 2013, pp. 139–143.

Demonstrating clarity of intent is also important. Because passing an authorization, itself, depends on public support (to the extent that members of Congress reflect their constituents' views), congressional authorization would signal purpose to the world actors whose help and support the United States seeks. It would also show clarity of resolve to the enemy.

On a deeper level, members of Congress, as the representatives of the American people, can give additional legitimacy to military operations by passing an authorization that reflects the will of their constituents. Inherently linked to the legitimacy of such an authorization is the public discussion that it entails. In this case, public support for U.S. counterterrorism strategy is an extremely valuable condition for lasting operational success. In general terms, that strategy should reflect the views of the American public. The process may be difficult and contentious, but such deliberations are an important part of the American democratic process.

Finally, congressional involvement in the development of U.S. counterterrorism strategy is desirable if for no other reason than to demonstrate that the United States values the important roles of both branches of government in foreign affairs. Congress declares war and controls the budget. The President is commander in chief and is responsible for carrying out foreign affairs. The nature of war as understood when the Constitution was drafted has evolved in some respects, but the U.S. system of checks and balances means that the nation's ability and authority to act are strongest when both branches of government act in unity.

One way of viewing the issue is that when the White House acts with congressional authorization, the legitimacy (and, hence, the power) of the President's actions is greater, both domestically and internationally, than it is without congressional endorsement. Some have argued that a President who acts with congressional support is backed by the "fullest extent" of presidential power.[43]

Thus, although the President may not require congressional authorization to use military force under most circumstances, most adminis-

---

[43] Bradley and Goldsmith, 2005, pp. 2050–2051.

trations would still prefer to have it. This preference is undoubtedly at the root of the White House's recent and occasionally confusing position on authorization, and it might explain the administration's back and forth on the issue over the course of 2013 and 2014.

Congressional authorizations do have some practical significance, of course. Even if the executive branch has the authority to use force without Congress, it will normally make an earnest effort to operate within congressionally authorized boundaries. It is simply politically safer to do so. U.S. counterterrorism operations since 9/11 have been made to fit the framework of the 2001 authorization. However, doing so has involved a significant amount of effort on the part of the executive branch legal staff.

The effect of authorization is ultimately therefore more akin to discouragement or encouragement of certain actions than it is to prohibition or prescription of those actions. This is one reason authorization is better for the U.S. military. Ultimately, the choice of whether or not to conduct a particular military operation is a matter of executive branch policy, though that policy may—to some degree—be informed by the congressional-legal framework.

Six Central Considerations

The main considerations in designing new legislation fall into six categories. In this section, we discuss the most desirable outcome, focusing in particular on those that relate to strategy rather than legal refinement. The six categories are geographical limitations, limits on ground forces, how groups or individuals are identified, the stated purposes for using force, reporting requirements, and sunset and renewal clauses.

It should be noted that crafting congressional authorization against terrorist groups is inherently difficult because of the nature of the groups themselves. Congress has authorized the use of military force against nonstate actors in the past, but in the 20th-century authorization was normally against state actors or their proxies.[44] These actors were naturally confined to a single, often contiguous geographical space and wore uniforms or were otherwise easily identifiable and fought for specific territorial or other objectives. Global terrorist organizations today, in contrast, are both geographically dispersed and diffuse in their membership, recruiting support over wide areas and often among civilian populations.

Geographical Limitations

Of the possible limitations Congress might seek to place on the executive branch's use of military power, geographical limitations make the least sense, because the adversary is not limited geographically in any meaningful way. Indeed, the very notion of what constitutes an international terrorist group includes actors and actions that transcend territorial bounds. The growth of ISIL far beyond Iraq and Syria demonstrates why limiting authorities to that area would be mistaken. New and dangerous ISIL affiliates are emerging in Libya, Yemen, the Sinai Peninsula, Afghanistan, and elsewhere. ISIL is attempting to rival its competition—al Qaeda—in terms of geographic spread. While it is reasonable to assume that the United States does not want to use military force everywhere ISIL establishes a foothold, in many places, it may need to. Under geographical limitations, the military would be hamstrung if operations become necessary in new and unforeseen areas.

A number of proposals have called for geographically limited authorizations. For example, House Joint Resolution (H.J. Res.) 125 states that "authority . . . shall be confined to the territory of the Republic of Iraq and the Syrian Arab Republic."[45] Similarly Senate Joint Resolution (S.J. Res.) 44 limits authority to operations in Iraq and, "if the

---

[44] Jennifer K. Elsea and Richard F. Grimmett, *Declarations of War and Authorizations for the Use of Military Force: Historical Background and Legal Implications*, Washington, D.C.: Congressional Research Service, March 2011.

[45] H.J. Res. 125, "Authorization for Use of Military Force Against ISIL Resolution," was introduced by Rep. Adam B. Schiff on September 16, 2014.

president deems necessary, in Syria."[46] Other proposals impose similar geographical restrictions.[47] The rationale given for such restrictions is that they will prevent the authorization from being used for unrelated conflicts.[48]

Neither al Qaeda nor ISIL, however, limit their operations to any single region. Since H.J. Res. 125 was introduced in the house, ISIL has strengthened its position in Egypt's Sinai Peninsula and established a major new foothold in Libya.[49] Boko Haram has pledged fealty to ISIL, and ISIL continues to seek recruits and allies elsewhere in the world. Al Qaeda, meanwhile, remains active in Sub-Saharan and North Africa, the Middle East, South Asia, and even the Asia-Pacific. This begs the question of whether the AUMF should be geographically limited when the enemies it targets are not. Secretary Kerry rightly argued in his December 2014 testimony that "it would be a mistake to advertise to ISIL that there are safe havens for them outside of Iraq and Syria" by way of an AUMF with geographical limitations. At the time of his testimony, however, Kerry also said that the administration "did not envisage" operations outside Iraq and Syria; yet, a mere two months later, there was widespread public debate over whether the war should be expanded to Libya in the face of ISIL's attacks there. These rapid changes reflect the problem with geographical limitations.

Several scholars have pointed out that just because an AUMF itself does not limit the use of force geographically, this does not rule out other types of geographical limitations. To begin with, there are the limits that any administration would impose on itself just as a matter of policy. Moreover, there are the limitations of international

---

[46] S.J. Res. 44, "Authorization for Use of Military Force Against the Islamic State in Iraq and the Levant," was introduced by Sen. Tim Kaine on September 17, 2014.

[47] See, for example, Ryan Goodman and Steve Vladeck, "Avoiding Unnecessary Wars and Preserving Accountability: Principles for an ISIL-Specific AUMF," *Just Security*, November 10, 2014. A similar restriction appears in Harold Hongju Koh, "The Lawful War to Fight the Islamic State," *Politico*, August 29, 2014.

[48] See, for example, Goodman and Vladeck, 2014.

[49] Louisa Loveluck and Magdy Samaan, "Dozens Dead in Egypt's Sinai as Islamists Launch Simultaneous Attacks," *The Telegraph*, January 29, 2015; Christopher S. Chivvis, "Countering the Islamic State in Libya," *Survival*, forthcoming..

norms and law. For this reason, several scholars have suggested including a reference to international law in the text of such an authorization document in place of a geographical limit.[50] This would have the effect of limiting the authorization to areas where there is a compelling need for operations without attempting to specify those areas in advance.

For these operational reasons, maximum geographic flexibility seems logical.

Limits on Ground Forces

It is not unprecedented that Congress might authorize military operations while limiting the military means available to the President for this purpose. The United States does not use all its tools of military power against terrorist organizations. Some of these tools (e.g., nuclear weapons) clearly have no place in counterterrorism operations.

Nevertheless, for obvious reasons, military operators would prefer the broadest possible remit in an authorization. In principle and practice, Congress defers to the executive branch for the day-to-day conduct of war. Its role is to authorize (or not) the use of force, not to determine the tactical details of a war's conduct. The requirements for successful military operations against terrorist groups cannot be foreseen in advance, and, from an operational perspective, it therefore seems unwise to tie the hands of military leaders in pursuit of objectives on which there is wide agreement. Moreover, the ability to signal that the United States is prepared to use larger-scale military force—including ground forces—is important to maintaining escalation dominance. This, in turn, should help put pressure on terrorist groups' support networks. From an operational perspective, these reasons would argue for the importance of keeping the possibility of even significant ground force deployments on the table.

For these reasons, imposing broad restrictions on the use of ground forces (or any other tools at the military's disposal) would also be counterproductive. Under such an AUMF, the U.S. military would be authorized to conduct a wide variety of operations, including shaping and training operations to strengthen local partners' abil-

---

[50] See, especially, Chesney et al., 2013.

ity to combat terrorist groups, operations directly supporting coalition partners, air and missile strikes, special operations, and intelligence, surveillance, and reconnaissance missions.

Few scholars favor ground force restrictions.[51] Injunctions on ground forces have nevertheless appeared in several proposals, including the White House's own. This is no doubt due to public reticence about ground force deployments after the frustrating experience of the Iraq War. H.J. Res. 125, for example, explicitly rules out the use of "ground forces in a combat role." Similarly, S.J. Res. 44 rules out "ground combat forces, except for [military assistance and training] or as necessary for the protection or rescue of members of the United States Armed Forces or United States citizens, . . . or for limited operations against high value targets." In the case of S.J. Res. 44, the limitation is less important, because that resolution would not repeal the 2001 legislation, which allows the use of ground forces. In the case of H.J. Res. 125, which would also repeal the 2001 AUMF, the limitation is far more serious.

The White House's proposed limits on "enduring offensive ground combat operations" have provoked much debate. The phrase has been widely interpreted to mean that the authorization would not cover anything akin to the war in Afghanistan or the 2003–2011 conflict in Iraq. This is obviously intended to make the legislation more palatable to an American public still deeply affected by those wars. Although public opinion can be fickle, at the time of this writing, it remained unfavorable to the deployment of ground forces in Iraq or Syria.[52] Hence, for the time being, at least, this limit simply reflects a political reality with which the White House would likely need to comply anyway. President Obama has repeatedly stated in the strongest terms that he has no intention to deploy such forces to engage in combat operations in Syria or Iraq. The limit thus appears to stem more from the desire to make legislation politically more palatable than any desire on the part of the

---

[51] The most prominent expert favoring ground force restrictions, at least as of summer 2014, was Harold Koh (see Koh, 2014). In contrast, neither Daskal and Vladeck (2014) nor Chesney et al. (2013) do so.

[52] See Pew Research Center, 2014.

administration to limit its own ability to wage war on ISIL—or any other terrorist organization.

In 2015, critics of the administration nevertheless seized on the phrase "enduring offensive ground combat operations" to argue that the White House is not truly committed to defeating ISIL. One claimed, for example, that the limit was "arbitrary" and "underscored the Obama administration's lack of seriousness" in its pursuit of the group.[53] But as many have pointed out, the language proposed by the administration does not limit the use of ground forces in any meaningful way. This is doubly true because the proposed legislation does not repeal the 2001 AUMF, which means the President could still use ground forces, even "enduring offensive ground combat operations" under that authorization.

The most logical basis for objections to the White House's non-limit limit is that a repeat of operations on the scale of the Iraq War may be necessary to defeat ISIL. In this case, the limit could discourage allies in the region hoping for another large-scale U.S. foray into Iraq. More important, such limits might encourage ISIL by demonstrating that the United States is unprepared to go to those lengths to defeat it.

But it is not yet clear that a repeat of the massive, multiyear, ground-heavy strategy used in Iraq from 2003 to 2011 will be the best way to defeat ISIL. Recent successes in Fallujah and Northern Iraq and Syria suggest that the gradual effort to degrade ISIL may be working, using a coalition approach, with a combination of airpower, special forces, careful intelligence work, and partner training efforts. There is also no reason to assume that a repeat of the Iraq War is what ISIL fears most.

How to Describe the Enemy
The question of how an AUMF should describe the enemy has two dimensions. The first is how broadly it should define the targeted groups. The second is how tightly it should circumscribe the use of force against those groups.

---

[53] John Yoo, "Say No to the AUMF," *National Review*, February 12, 2015.

The first of these questions, how broadly to define the groups targeted, is about whether to specify al Qaeda, ISIL, or any other specific groups in the legislation. Doing so has the value of clarifying U.S. strategic objectives. Some definition of the enemy seems a reasonable expectation, but finding specific terminology that accurately describes today's threat—without the need for perpetual updates going forward—will be difficult.

The 2001 AUMF does not refer to al Qaeda specifically but instead authorizes the use of force against "nations, organizations, or persons [the President] determines planned, authorized, committed, or aided the terrorist attacks that occurred on September 11, 2001, or harbored such organizations or persons." This language describes the enemy that the United States faced 14 years ago and not the threat it faces today.

The February 2015 White House draft AUMF defines *associated forces* broadly as "individuals and organizations fighting for, on behalf of, or alongside ISIL or any closely-related successor entity in hostilities against the United States or its coalition partners."[54] Some scholars have criticized this as too broad a definition,[55] but the evolution of terrorist groups demonstrates the changing nature of relationships between the core and periphery and between new and old terrorist groups. And adequate reporting requirements might serve to reduce otherwise high levels of concern about a somewhat broader definition of associated forces. Jeh Johnson, in a speech shortly before he departed DoD, described *associated forces* as "an organized, armed group that has entered the fight alongside al Qaeda, cobelligerent with al Qaeda in hostilities against the U.S. or its coalition partners."[56] DoD general counsel Stephen Preston referenced the definition in an April 2015 speech on the AUMF.[57]

---

[54] See Obama, 2015.

[55] See, for example, Ryan Goodman, "Obama's Forever War Starts Today," *Foreign Policy*, February 12, 2015.

[56] Jeh Johnson, "National Security Law, Lawyers and Lawyering in the Obama Administration," lecture, Yale Law School, February 22, 2012.

[57] Jim Garamone, "General Counsel Charts Use of Force Law's Evolution," U.S. Department of Defense, April 13, 2015.

Given the diverse and changing nature of the threat, relatively broad language will be necessary. It is important to note that just because a group is covered under an authorization, that does not necessarily mean that the United States will use force against it. What it means is that the United States considers itself justified, for reasons of national security, in using force against that group, should the need arise.

The second question of how tightly to circumscribe the use of force against the targeted groups has to do with the extent to which the United States will use force against individuals and groups that aid and abet terrorists. Clearly, the United States would authorize the use of force against core members of a given group—those who conduct, lead, and or otherwise play a central role in plotting terrorist attacks. But would the United States use force against the group's fundraisers, recruiters, and other facilitators?

This question becomes particularly thorny when considering strategies to combat ISIL, which is running a quasi-state that relies on the support of many "volunteers." Should those who run food banks or schools in Syria in ISIL-controlled territories be considered associates of the group? Clearly not, and doing so would stretch the definition too far.

For these reasons, a certain degree of ambiguity in an AUMF may be desirable. It would also be counterproductive public messaging to telegraph that the United States intends to target anyone who can be linked in any way to terrorist organizations; after all, many of these people may not be acting under their own free will.

Yet, there is deterrent value in making it clear that some types of support to terrorist groups may be met with lethal force. It is common practice in wartime for states to target the financial and economic infrastructure of enemies with military force, and those who provide that infrastructure to terrorist groups should be forced to operate under similarly risky conditions. Congress may wish to bear this in mind during its deliberations. In practice, of course, the executive branch will determine on a case-by-case basis whether to use force against those who support terrorist organizations, but whoever is in the White

House will be better off if they have congressional backing when doing so.

Given these issues, Congress might decide that, operationally, the best option is a straightforward AUMF "against international terrorist groups the President deems a serious threat to the security of the nation." As needed, the documentation could describe the attributes of terrorist groups that pose a serious threat to the nation's security or might in the future. It could also include the stated intent and describe the potential capability to attack the homeland, language initially suggested by former DoD general counsel and current Secretary of Homeland Security Jeh Johnson.[58]

Congress might choose such an approach to telegraph the clear intent of the United States to combat global terrorist threats regardless of moniker, religious affiliation, or ideological basis, putting the focus on the nature of the threat rather than the nature of the group.

If so, the administration would need to specify the groups targeted via the AUMF reporting requirement, as described in the next section. When combined with a renewal clause and, possibly, some

---

[58] In a lecture at Yale Law School in February 2012, Johnson stated that

> the AUMF, the statutory authorization from 2001, is not open-ended. It does not authorize military force against anyone the executive labels a "terrorist." Rather, it encompasses only those groups or people with a link to the terrorist attacks on 9/11, or associated forces.
>
> Nor is the concept of an "associated force" an open-ended one, as some suggest. This concept, too, has been upheld by the courts in the detention context, and it is based on the well-established concept of co-belligerency in the law of war. The concept has become more relevant over time, as al Qaeda has, over the last 10 years, become more de-centralized, and relies more on associates to carry out its terrorist aims.
>
> An "associated force," as we interpret the phrase, has two characteristics to it: (1) an organized, armed group that has entered the fight alongside al Qaeda, and (2) is a co-belligerent with al Qaeda in hostilities against the United States or its coalition partners. In other words, the group must not only be aligned with al Qaeda. It must have also entered the fight against the United States or its coalition partners. Thus, an "associated force" is not any terrorist group in the world that merely embraces the al Qaeda ideology. More is required before we draw the legal conclusion that the group fits within the statutory authorization for the use of military force passed by the Congress in 2001. (Johnson, 2012)

limits on the methods of force to be applied, Congress might well view a broad definition of the threat as appropriate.

The Purposes for Which Military Force Is to Be Used

Specifying the purposes for which military force may be used is possibly the most important aspect of AUMF legislation because it can both limit and legitimize the use of force. Also, military commanders often note that their job is easier when they are given clear objectives by their political leadership.

The White House's proposed counter-ISIL legislation does not specify a purpose and has been rightly criticized for that omission. (In other statements, however, the President has described U.S. objectives as being to "degrade, and ultimately destroy" ISIL through a broad counterterrorism strategy.) H.J. Res. 125, which limits presidential authority in other ways, does not specify a purpose for which force might be used. A draft AUMF proposed by several leading scholars also lacks such a statement of purpose, even though some of the same scholars have argued that a statement of purpose is important.[59]

Clearly, the central and potentially most important purpose for which military force will be used is to prevent imminent attacks on the U.S. homeland. However, military force will often be most effective when used against groups early in their development. There is consensus among counterterrorism experts that it is far better to counter a group early in its growth phase than to wait for it to metastasize into a full-blown regional and global threat. There is also broad agreement that the way to disrupt a terrorist network is to exert persistent pressure over time. Therefore, Congress may decide to provide the military with the flexibility to conduct operations not only to prevent imminent threats but also to take various types of actions against terrorist groups early in their development to deflect and thwart their potential future threat.

---

[59] Compare Benjamin Wittes, Robert Chesney, Jack Goldsmith, and Matthew Waxman, "A Draft AUMF to Get the Discussion Going," *Lawfare Blog*, November 10, 2015, and Jack Goldsmith, Steve Vladeck, and Ryan Goodman, "Six Questions Congress Should Ask the Administration About Its ISIL AUMF," *Lawfare Blog*, February 20, 2015.

Assuming this broad remit, three qualifications seem desirable. First, it may be worth signaling that military force is part of a broader whole-of-government approach, indicating to the world that the United States does not believe it can effectively combat terrorists with military force alone. Second, reference could be made to conducting operations in such a way that strengthens international security and the rule of law. Third, it may be desirable to add reference to the need for U.S. military operations to comply with international law.

Language that included these elements would look something like the following, authorizing the use of force

> as part of a multidimensional U.S. strategy to degrade and dismantle terrorist organizations to ensure that they can no longer credibly threaten the security of the United States, its allies, or populations in the regions in which they operate. The United States will pursue these objectives with full respect for international law and with the broader aim of strengthening international security and the rule of law worldwide.

Reporting Requirements

Congress may find broad language to describe the targeted groups and their associates in any AUMF to be preferable for the reasons argued earlier in this report. However, Congress may also choose to specify the groups against which the authorization is currently being used in order to inform the public and single out the most dangerous enemies to U.S. national security. One appealing option would be to require the executive branch to report to Congress on a regular basis, identifying the groups that it considers to be authorized by the language of the law.[60]

The current draft provided by the White House stipulates that the President must report to Congress at least once every six months "on specific actions taken pursuant to this authorization."[61] While that frequency of reporting is reasonable, the content is unspecified, and the term *specific action* needs clarification.

---

[60] See also Jack Goldsmith, "Why a Substantively Neutral but Procedurally Constraining AUMF Makes Sense," *Lawfare Blog*, November 11, 2014.

[61] Obama, 2015, p. 3.

Among the most important details that could be reported to Congress is the list of targeted groups. While discussions of the rationale for targeting these groups could be classified, the list of the groups would be publicly available.

In these reports, some general, strategic information may be sufficient for the unclassified, public version. Reporting could also be backward-looking—addressing operations that have been conducted consistent with the authorization—as opposed to forward-looking reporting outlining what the executive branch is planning to do. Reporting on what has happened in the prior six months would be sufficient to indicate how the authorization is being interpreted and applied.

One of the benefits of a national discussion of counterterrorism operations is that the alphabet soup of groups that do or might pose a threat to the United States can sometimes confound the public. It can be unclear exactly which groups the executive branch believes rise to the level of threat requiring a military response. It would also help counter enemy propaganda efforts. The U.S. Department of State maintains a list of foreign terrorist organizations against which sanctions and other tools of foreign policy are regularly applied, but the groups against which military force is authorized would be only a small subset of this much longer list. Except in very rare circumstances, there is no reason for the administration to keep the names of groups that have already been targeted out of the public eye. Being off the list could even have a deterrent effect for groups considering more aggressive action against the United States.

For these reasons, most experts favor reporting requirements of some kind.[62] H.J. Res 44 calls for reports every 90 days, a period that could become onerous due to the short time frame. Moreover, the frequency of public and classified reports need not be the same. For example, the unclassified, public report could be issued on an annual basis, while a classified report to Congress could be released every six months.

---

[62] Goldsmith, Vladeck, and Goodman, 2015; Wittes, 2015; Koh, 2014; Jennifer Daskal and Benjamin Wittes, "The Intellectual—but Not the Political—AUMF Consensus," *Just Security*, March 2, 2015.

This would not preclude the executive branch from voluntarily updating the list in the interim. Every effort should be made, of course, to ensure that the requirements are straightforward and not onerous.

Sunset and Renewal

One of the primary objections to the war that followed the 2001 authorization was that it has no end. It is never clear at the outset when wars will end, and, historically, wars often last longer than expected. In this case, because of the nebulous nature of the enemy, it is unlikely that the conflict will end with a definitive military victory. Given this, concerns that the United States could be engaged in a "forever war" are not groundless.

However, the United States will be engaged with some array of terrorist adversaries for a long time to come, and the enemy and the military requirements needed to address it will change. The law that authorizes these military operations should therefore be periodically revisited. This should not be confused with setting a date on which hostilities will end or military force will no longer be needed. The purpose of a renewal clause would instead be to establish a schedule for revisiting the need for and types of force to be used.

Recourse to the military tool should be a function of the level of threat the nation faces. The point at which the terrorist threat has been reduced to a level at which military operations are no longer needed— or a different set of military tools are needed—may be a long way off, but it is right to keep that expectation at the forefront of discussion and debate. Continuing military operations beyond the point at which they serve a clear purpose would obviously be a waste of precious military, financial, political, and moral resources.

That said, some experts have advocated an open-ended authorization on the grounds that to do otherwise would impose "arbitrary deadlines" on a war or otherwise encourage the enemy.[63] These objections treat a renewal clause as a deadline or termination date when it is much better viewed as a reinvigoration of the authority. If a war is progressing in such a way that Congress is unable to agree to renew the

---

[63] Yoo, 2015.

authorization, then the authorization has already lost most of its meaning. Even in this case, however, the executive branch might choose to continue to prosecute the war, relying on its other authorities. Nevertheless, there is a risk inherent in opening the authorization to debate and renewal three years down the road, when both political and security circumstances will have changed. Establishing this sunset, then, involves some risk that Congress will refuse to reauthorize when the fight is not over. Harold Koh rightly points out that this is a risk worth taking:

> [A] sunset is not a repeal; it need not even be read as a proposal to repeal in the future. Just look at the renewals of the Patriot Act. A sunset is simply a shared congressional-executive agreement to reassess the situation together as a nation sometime in 2018, 17 years after 9/11, when we will have a new president and congress, and have a much better sense of whether our war effort against ISIL has made progress.[64]

Renewal clauses may be desirable for at least two reasons. First, the terrorist threat is dynamic and changing. As we have seen in the past, there can be major shifts in the nature of the terrorist threat. Examples include al Qaeda's spread into new territory followed by the rise, competition, and ultimate expulsion of one affiliate (AQI) and its transformation into an entity—ISIL. Now independent from al Qaeda, ISIL is a very dangerous but different kind of enemy from the one envisioned when the original authorization was drafted.

Second, renewal clauses can enhance the overall legitimacy of the legislation, not least by ensuring continued public discussion of the significance of the threat. They do not necessarily mean that an authorization will not be extended—only that it will be reconsidered and voted on again, thereby giving Congress the opportunity to convey its understanding of both the changing strategic environment and evolving public opinion. There is no reason to assume that a renewal debate will necessarily result in a restriction on authority. Indeed, renewal

---

[64] Harold Koh, "Sunset and Supersede: Striking the Right Balance in the AUMF Against ISIL," *Just Security*, March 2015.

could even be an opportunity to strengthen the authorization, if necessary, in response to changes in the threat environment. In the long run, the goal is that it would be a reflection of the fact that the threat itself had diminished.

One argument against including a sunset provision stems from concerns that groups will take some measure of comfort in thinking that U.S. resolve is temporary and they need only to persevere until the expiration of the AUMF. Of course, Congress could decide to revise or renew the legislation rather than allowing it to expire without action. In either case, if Congress were concerned about sending such a message, the language of a sunset clause could be clear that it reflects the need to revisit the authorization and does not necessarily dictate the end of a conflict.

Possible Directions and Implications

The preceding six considerations should inform the development of any AUMF framework. Procedurally, there are different ways in which such a framework might be enacted.

First, Congress could simply repeal existing legislation and pass one omnibus authorization that meets all these requirements. This would send a clear affirmation of U.S. commitment to future counterterrorism operations, reduce the temptation to introduce piecemeal authorization resolutions, and offer a more clear and rational overall framework for counterterrorism needs.

Second, as was requested by the Obama administration, Congress might pass a new authorization specifically for operations against ISIL, taking no action on counterterrorism more broadly, including reform of the 2001 authorization. If the counter-ISIL legislation included most of the provisions noted here (it could not, by definition, include all of them, such as the broad definition of forces and purposes), this would likely be better than no congressional action at all because it would add legitimacy to operations against the growing ISIL threat. It would still be an incomplete reform, however, since it would presumably leave the 2001 authorization in place. The United States would be slightly better positioned in its fight against ISIL, thanks to congressional action, but many of the questions that have dogged the 2001 authorization in recent years would remain.

A third option would be for Congress to pass the counter-ISIL authorization and consider updating or repealing the 2001 legislation at a later date. Updating or repealing the 2001 legislation would serve as a foundation for U.S. counterterrorism operations in the longer term, while the counter-ISIL legislation could be viewed as an exceptional case above and beyond the foundational legislation, reflecting the exceptional nature of the current threat from ISIL. On the whole, however, Congress might find a dual-track solution to be more trouble than it would be worth, since the required authorities for operations against the two groups are ultimately so similar.

A fourth option would be for Congress to pass counter-ISIL legislation and repeal the 2001 authorization. This could have the unintended effect of signaling that Congress believes that al Qaeda is no longer a threat. In some ways, al Qaeda may be a greater long-term threat to the United States than ISIL.[65]

A fifth option would be for Congress to decline to pass new legislation or fail to take action altogether. In that case, the executive branch would likely continue using the 2001 AUMF as its authority to conduct operations against ISIL in Iraq and Syria, as well as its continuing operations against al Qaeda and its affiliates. This legislative outcome might come about for several reasons: Many critics see Obama's draft authorization as too narrow, constricting the President's freedom of action.[66] Others find that the draft provides too few restrictions on how the administration will prosecute counterterrorism operations, defines the enemy too broadly, and fails to adequately explain what the use of force would achieve. Key Senate Democrats have said that they

---

[65] Eric Schmitt, "ISIS or Al Qaeda? American Officials Split Over Top Terror Threat," *New York Times*, August 4, 2015.

[66] Daniel Newhuaser, "Why Obama's AUMF Faces Trouble on the Hill," *National Journal*, February 11, 2015.

would not vote for the President's draft bill if it came to a vote as is.[67] The Republican leadership equally opposes such a bill as too restrictive and has ruled out any additional limitations. Some Republican congressional leaders, moreover, object to the congressional role in such authorizations altogether—a view, for example, put forward by Senator Lindsey Graham during the debate over authorization for the 2011 Libya campaign.

Ultimately, the failure to pass a new AUMF would have little operational impact. The administration and any future administration could continue operations against ISIL, al Qaeda, and other terrorist groups, for all the reasons described here. But leaving the legislation as it is risks demonstrating to both allies and enemies a difficulty on the part of the executive and legislative branches to speak in unison about how to defeat current and future terrorist threats. This could too easily reinforce the view among U.S. allies and enemies that Washington is passing through a particularly dysfunctional period in its politics. The problem of extremist groups with lethal capabilities is not going away. By passing a new AUMF, Congress could, if it chooses, make it clear that the United States will stand up to terrorist groups, sees defeating them as vital to national security, and is prepared to pay the price.

---

[67] Manu Raju and Burgess Everett, "War Authorization in Trouble on Hill," *Politico*, March 15, 2015.

References

Berger, J. M., "The Islamic State vs. al Qaeda," *Foreign Policy*, September 2, 2014.

Bradley, Curtis A., and Jack L. Goldsmith, "Congressional Authorization and the War on Terrorism," *Harvard Law Review*, Vol. 118, No. 7, May 2005, pp. 2047–2133.

Byman, Daniel, and Jennifer Williams, "ISIS vs. Al Qaeda: Jihadism's Global Civil War," *National Interest*, February 24, 2015.

Chesney, Robert, Jack Goldsmith, Matthew C. Waxman, and Benjamin Wittes, *A Statutory Framework for Next Generation Terrorist Threats*, Hoover Institution, 2013.

Chivvis, Christopher S., *Toppling Qaddafi: Libya and the Limits of Liberal Intervention*, New York: Cambridge University Press, 2013.

———, "Countering the Islamic State in Libya," *Survival*, forthcoming.

Cohen, David, "John McCain: Don't Handcuff President," *Politico*, February 15, 2015. As of June 14, 2015:
http://www.politico.com/story/2015/02/mccain-dont-handcuff-president-115218.html

Daschle, Tom, "Power We Didn't Grant," *Washington Post*, December 23, 2005.

Daskal, Jennifer, and Stephen I. Vladeck, "After the AUMF," *Harvard National Security Journal*, Vol. 5, 2014, pp. 115–146.

Daskal, Jennifer, and Benjamin Wittes, "The Intellectual—but Not the Political—AUMF Consensus," *Just Security*, March 2, 2015. As of June 14, 2015:
http://justsecurity.org/20546/intellectual-but-political-aumf-consensus/

Elsea, Jennifer K., and Richard F. Grimmett, *Declarations of War and Authorizations for the Use of Military Force: Historical Background and Legal Implications*, Washington, D.C.: Congressional Research Service, March 2011.

French, Bill, and John Bradshaw, *Ending the Endless War*, Washington, D.C.: National Security Network, August 2014.

Garamone, Jim, "General Counsel Charts Use of Force Law's Evolution," U.S. Department of Defense, April 13, 2015. As of June 14, 2015:
http://www.defense.gov/news/newsarticle.aspx?id=128573

Goldsmith, Jack, "Why a Substantively Neutral but Procedurally Constraining AUMF Makes Sense," *Lawfare Blog*, November 11, 2014. As of June 14, 2015:
http://www.lawfareblog.com/
why-substantively-neutral-procedurally-constraining-aumf-makes-sense

———, "The Administration's Hard-to-Fathom Draft AUMF," *Lawfare Blog*, February 12, 2015. As of June 14, 2015:
http://www.lawfareblog.com/administration's-hard-fathom-draft-aumf

Goldsmith, Jack, Steve Vladeck, and Ryan Goodman, "Six Questions Congress Should Ask the Administration About Its ISIL AUMF," *Lawfare Blog*, February 20, 2015. As of June 14, 2015:
http://www.lawfareblog.com/
six-questions-congress-should-ask-administration-about-its-isil-aumf

Goodman, Ryan, "Obama's Forever War Starts Today," *Foreign Policy*, February 12, 2015.

Goodman, Ryan, and Steve Vladeck, "Avoiding Unnecessary Wars and Preserving Accountability: Principles for an ISIL-Specific AUMF," *Just Security*, November 10, 2014. As of June 14, 2015:
http://justsecurity.org/17257/aumf-principles/

Greenwald, Glenn, "Barbara Lee and Dick Durbin's 'Nobody-Could-Have-Known' Defense," *The Guardian*, May 7, 2013.

House Joint Resolution 125, Authorization for the Use of Military Force Against ISIL Resolution, 113th Congress, September 16, 2014.

"In AUMF Hearing, Kaine Renews Call for Swift, Bipartisan Congressional Action and Presses for Clarity on Ground Troops," press release, March 11, 2015. As of June 14, 2015:
http://www.kaine.senate.gov/press-releases/in-aumf-hearing-kaine-renews-call-for-swift-bipartisan-congressional-action-and-presses-for-clarity-on-ground-troops

Ingram, David, "U.S. War on al Qaeda Is Not Indefinite—Pentagon Lawyer," Reuters, December 1, 2012. As of June 14, 2015:
http://in.reuters.com/article/2012/12/01/
usa-qaeda-johnson-idINDEE8AT0HN20121201

Johnson, Jeh, General Counsel, U.S. Department of Defense, "National Security Law, Lawyers and Lawyering in the Obama Administration," lecture, Yale Law School, February 22, 2012.

Jones, Seth G., *A Persistent Threat: The Evolution of al Qa'ida and Other Salafi Jihadists*, Santa Monica, Calif.: RAND Corporation, RR-637-OSD, 2014. As of June 14, 2015:
http://www.rand.org/pubs/research_reports/RR637.html

Kerry, John, Secretary of State, statement before the Committee on Foreign Relations, U.S. Senate, at the hearing "Authorization to Use Force Against ISIL," December 9, 2014.

Koh, Harold Hongju, "The Lawful War to Fight the Islamic State," *Politico*, August 29, 2014. As of June 14, 2015:
http://www.politico.com/magazine/story/2014/08/the-lawful-way-to-fight-the-islamic-state-110444.html

———, "Sunset and Supersede: Striking the Right Balance in the AUMF Against ISIL," *Just Security*, March 2015. As of June 14, 2015:
http://justsecurity.org/20570/
sunset-supersede-striking-balance-authorization-military-force-aumf-isil

Kroenig Matthew H., and Barry Pavel, "How to Deter Terrorism," *Washington Quarterly*, Spring 2012.

Laub, Zachary, and Jonathan Masters, *The Islamic State*, backgrounder, New York: Council on Foreign Relations, May 18, 2015. As of June 14, 2015:
http://www.cfr.org/iraq/islamic-state/p14811

Loveluck, Louisa, and Magdy Samaan, "Dozens Dead in Egypt's Sinai as Islamists Launch Simultaneous Attacks," *The Telegraph*, January 29, 2015.

National Counterterrorism Center, "Al Qa'ida in the Arabian Peninsula (AQAP)," *Counterterrorism Guide*, undated(a). As of June 14, 2015:
http://www.nctc.gov/site/groups/aqap.html

———, "Islamic State of Iraq and the Levant (ISIL)," *Counterterrorism Guide*, undated(b). As of June 14, 2015:
http://www.nctc.gov/site/groups/aqi_isil.html

Newhuaser, Daniel, "Why Obama's AUMF Faces Trouble on the Hill," National Journal, February 11, 2015.

Obama, Barack, "Joint Resolution to Authorize the Limited Use of the United States Armed Forces in Against the Islamic State of Iraq and the Levant," draft authorization, February 11, 2015. As of June 14, 2015:
https://www.whitehouse.gov/sites/default/files/docs/aumf_02112015.pdf

O'Brien, Lauren B., "The Evolution of Terrorism Since 9/11," *FBI Law Enforcement Bulletin*, September 2011. As of October 5, 2015:
https://leb.fbi.gov/2011/september/the-evolution-of-terrorism-since-9-11

Olsen, Matthew G., director, National Counterterrorism Center, statement before the Committee on Homeland Security, U.S. House of Representatives, at the hearing "Worldwide Threats to the Homeland," September 17, 2014.

O'Toole, Molly, "Obama to Ask Congress for New War Powers to Fight ISIS," *Defense One*, November 5, 2014. As of June 14, 2015:
http://www.defenseone.com/politics/2014/11/
obama-ask-congress-new-war-powers-fight-isis/98270/

Paul, Christopher, Colin P. Clarke, Beth Grill, Stephanie Young, Jennifer D. P. Moroney, Joe Hogler, and Christine Leah, *What Works Best When Building Partner Capacity and Under What Circumstances?* Santa Monica, Calif.: RAND Corporation, MG-1253/1-OSD, 2013. As of October 5, 2015: http://www.rand.org/pubs/monographs/MG1253z1.html

Pew Research Center, "Support for U.S. Campaign Against ISIS; Doubts About Its Effectiveness, Objectives," October 2014. As of June 14, 2015: http://www.people-press.org/2014/10/22/ support-for-u-s-campaign-against-isis-doubts-about-its-effectiveness-objectives

Public Law 107-40, Joint Resolution to Authorize the Use of United States Armed Forces Against Those Responsible for the Recent Attacks Launched Against the United States, September 18, 2001.

Public Law 107-243, Authorization for Use of Military Force Against Iraq Resolution of 2002, October 16, 2002.

Raju, Manu, and Burgess Everett, "War Authorization in Trouble on Hill," *Politico*, March 15, 2015. As of June 14, 2015: http://www.politico.com/story/2015/03/no-clear-way-forward-isil-war-authorization-115773.html

Rasmussen, Nicholas J., director, National Counterterrorism Center, statement before the Select Committee on Intelligence, U.S. Senate, at the hearing "Current Terrorist Threat to the United States," February 12, 2015.

"Repeal the Military Force Law," *New York Times*, March 9, 2013.

Senate Joint Resolution 44, Authorization for Use of Military Force Against the Islamic State in Iraq and the Levant, 113th Congress, September 17, 2014.

Schmitt, Eric, "ISIS or Al Qaeda? American Officials Split Over Top Terror Threat," *New York Times*, August 4, 2015.

Shapiro, Jacob N., *The Terrorist's Dilemma: Managing Violent Covert Organizations*, Princeton, N.J.: Princeton University Press, 2013.

"Views from Washington: The Changing Terrorist Threat," video of discussion with Matthew Olsen at Harvard Law School, October 8, 2014. As of June 14, 2015: https://www.youtube.com/watch?v=XTpn4J8oG2E

Weiss, Michael, and Hassan Hassan, *Inside the Army of Terror*, New York: Reagan Arts, 2015.

White House, "Remarks by the President at the National Defense University," transcript, May 23, 2013. As of June 14, 2015: http://www.whitehouse.gov/the-press-office/2013/05/23/ remarks-president-national-defense-university

Wittes, Benjamin, senior fellow, Brookings Institution, statement before the Committee on Armed Forces, U.S. House of Representatives, at the hearing "Outside Perspectives on the President's Proposed Authorization for the Use of Military Force Against the Islamic State of Iraq and the Levant," February 26, 2015.

Wittes, Benjamin, Robert Chesney, Jack Goldsmith, and Matthew Waxman, "A Draft AUMF to Get the Discussion Going," *Lawfare Blog*, November 10, 2015. As of June 14, 2015:
http://www.lawfareblog.com/draft-aumf-get-discussion-going

Yoo, John, "Say No to the AUMF," *National Review*, February 12, 2015. As of June 14, 2015:
http://www.nationalreview.com/article/413680/say-no-aumf-john-yoo

Zelin, Aaron Y., "Al-Qaeda Disaffiliates with the Islamic State of Iraq and al-Sham," policy alert, Washington, D.C.: Washington Institute, February 4, 2014. As of June 14, 2015:
http://www.washingtoninstitute.org/policy-analysis/view/al-qaeda-disaffiliates-with-the-islamic-state-of-iraq-and-al-sham

———, *The Islamic State: A Video Introduction*, Washington, D.C.: Washington Institute for Near East Policy, January 13, 2015.